THE
BLACK REPORT

Charting the Changing Status of African Americans

**Inaugural Edition
1997**

Billy J. Tidwell

**DataDeeds, LLP.
and
University Press of America, Inc.**
Lanham • New York • Oxford

Copyright © 1997 by
University Press of America,® Inc.
4720 Boston Way
Lanham, Maryland 20706

12 Hid's Copse Rd.
Cummor Hill, Oxford OX2 9JJ

Library of Congress Cataloging-in-Publication Data

Tidwell, Billy J.
The Black report: charting the changing status of African Americans /
Billy J. Tidwell.--Inaugural ed.
p.   cm.
l. Afro-Americans--Social conditions--1975--Statistics. I. Title.
E185.86.T49   1997   305.896'073--dc21   96-40368 CIP

ISBN 0-7618-0682-2 (cloth: alk. ppr.)
ISBN 0-7618-0683-0 (pbk: alk. ppr.)

TABLE OF CONTENTS

LIST OF FIGURES

I. BLACK DEMOGRAPHICS

II. BLACK HEALTH

III. BLACK EDUCATION

IV. BLACK ECONOMICS

V. BLACK POLITICAL EMPOWERMENT

VI. BLACK YOUTH

Race: 1996

LIST OF TABLES

I. BLACK DEMOGRAPHICS

II. BLACK HEALTH

III. BLACK EDUCATION

IV. BLACK ECONOMICS

V. BLACK POLITICAL EMPOWERMENT

VI. BLACK YOUTH

PREFACE

What are the numbers, and what do they say? In this time of fiscal austerity and growing social problems, these have become increasingly urgent questions. No longer is it prudent or productive to rely upon intuition and impressionistic observation as a basis for drawing inferences about human needs and responses to them. The point takes on special significance as one considers the complex, changing condition of African Americans. So much has been achieved, yet so much remains to be done to realize the improvement in life circumstances that is so long overdue them. But the odds against redress have risen starkly in recent years, thanks to political activists who would consign racial justice to the back burner of the nation's priorities. All of this demands more intensive empirical analyses of where Black America is, where it seems to be headed, and the choices that might accomplish beneficial redirections in the face of regressive opposition.

With the publication of its inaugural edition of *The Black Report*, **DataDeeds** seeks to aid the assessment-response process. The work is geared to all of those organizations and individuals--public and private--who would serve the well-being of the black community in some area, whether it be education, employment, family functioning, or others that bear directly upon quality of life. The publication is multi-purpose, both in the subject matter covered and in the ways in which it can be used. It is our sincere hope that its potential will be fully utilized.

President & CEO
Billy J. Tidwell, Ph.D.

ACKNOWLEDGMENTS

A number of people contributed to the successful completion of this book. Special thanks to Barbara Harris for her advice and guidance on the use of census data. Her assistance was extremely helpful throughout. Thanks, also, to Mia Roberts, Sam Johnson, and Djenaba Tidwell for reviewing and commenting upon the draft manuscript. Their critical input was thoughtful and illuminating. Similarly, my deepest gratitude to Johnnie Griffin, who meticulously and proficiently edited the entire document, which made for a significantly better final product. Marcus Gordon and his company, Datex, performed an equally expert job in technically integrating the various components of the work and preparing it to go to press. Finally, I must acknowledge the longstanding support of my parents, Edgar (deceased) and Verdalia Tidwell. Their encouragement and sacrifices are ultimately responsible for the professional success I have achieved, including publication of *The Black Report*.

INTRODUCTION

This report profiles the Black America of the 1990s in various dimensions. It grew out of the mounting concerns about the present character of African-American life and anxiety over rapidly deteriorating possibilities for the future. The situation demands more critical, objective assessment of status and directions. The situation requires sound empirical understanding of the African-American condition.

Of course, there is no simple way to tell the story of Black Americans. Their history is complex and highly eventful. From slavery to Jim Crow to the civil rights era to the age of equal opportunity, the black experience has been a multifaceted, sharply visible part of the American scene. And through the changing sociopolitical contexts, the challenges to black survival and well-being have severely tested the group's resolve, resilience, and resourcefulness. Given the oppressive constraints, the advancement blacks have made over the generations is truly remarkable. In both absolute terms and relative to the majority white population, blacks have made tremendous gains in education, employment, income, and other vital areas of socioeconomic status.

Nonetheless, even in the contemporary period, blacks cannot take their collective progress for granted. To the contrary, there are new conditions and forces in play that are frustrating present aspirations and threatening the welfare of coming generations.

Most significantly, there has been a widespread resurgence of political conservatism in the country. Across the body politic, there is much less support for social programs to assist blacks and other disadvantaged minorities than existed in previous times. And one of the policies that has done most to narrow racial inequalities, affirmative action, is under fierce attack from the right. Although the Clinton Administration in its first term opposed the wholesale dismantling of affirmative action initiatives, it nonetheless made strategic concessions to retrenchment. Worse, the Supreme Court, long a champion of racial justice, has recently rendered decisions that effectively set back the clock. In California, the November elections brought the passage of Proposition 209, a controversial measure that abolishes the use of racial and gender preferences. Thus the prospects for affirmative action at this point are very much in doubt.

Concomitant with the new political conservatism, racial intolerance has reached new heights. One need look no further than the rash of black church burnings that went unchecked for more than two years. While not all of these cases can be called acts of racism, it is clear that the general reactionary atmosphere was a principal contributing factor. Blacks and all right-thinking Americans have good reason to be profoundly disturbed by the chain of events and equally discouraged by the limited success of law enforcement agencies in apprehending the perpetrators and deterring the recurrence of such unconscionable offenses.

There is also ongoing concern about the impacts of the changed national economy on the black community. From the inexorable decline of manufacturing industries to the rapid ascendancy of corporate downsizing, black workers enjoy substantially less economic opportunity and security than before and are finding it much more difficult to establish and sustain an economic foothold for themselves and their families. In fact, the corporate downsizing trend has wreaked havoc among middle-class African Americans whose hard work, dedication, and educational attainment, they believed, had rewarded them with a comfortable position in the economic mainstream. Instead, disproportionate numbers of this highly educated, highly skilled group have found themselves displaced by the new competitive forces in the marketplace. Many have rebounded from the misfortune by accepting significantly lower paying, less prestigious jobs than they lost.

Of course, blacks with limited education and skills continue to be particularly hard hit by transformations in the manufacturing sector and the escalating technical demands of the modern economy. This segment of the African-American workforce has few options in the present and faces an increasingly bleak economic future. Far too many black youth find themselves in this circumstance--marginalized.

The condition of black youth deserves further comment, for they have become a growing menace to themselves and their own communities. Youth violence by and against blacks is among the most distressing phenomena of our day. Rampant drug use, the proliferation of gang activity, and a value system that seemingly disregards the sanctity of human life head the characteristics that spell nihilism from within. And, of course, the larger public's insistence on increased law enforcement, harsher sentences, and more prisons to house the offenders has not been balanced by a commitment to progressive programs that would offer needy black youth viable alternatives to destructiveness.

These are some of the troubling developments that jeopardize the collective well-being of Black Americans as we move into the new century. They represent serious challenges, and strong measures must be taken to check and reverse the disquieting trends, particularly by Black Americans themselves.

Indeed, the black community has no choice but to organize, mobilize, and exercise its energies and resources for the collective good, invoking the strong tradition of self-help and group enterprise that has distinguished its history. In this regard, the Million Man March was a powerful demonstration that the tradition is still alive. Overlooking the political side issues, the March showed that inspiring leadership, skillful organizing, and effective promotion can tap the wellsprings of potential that exist in today's Black America. On a lesser scale, there are countless impressive models of collective effort all across the nation--Black Americans doing for themselves to realize a better way of life. Although they do not command widespread public attention, these community-based activities, en toto, comprise an essential infrastructure upon which to build and operationalize broader institutional initiatives.

This is not to say that the black community alone is capable of solving all of the formidable problems it confronts. Many of them are of such magnitude and complexity as to defy a strictly self-reliant approach. In other words, black self-help is necessary but insufficient to achieve *"the dream."* There is an indispensable role for government in the process. The other part of the strategy for black progress, then, is for blacks to exert the full extent of their collective political power to have the government fulfill its legitimate responsibility for realizing racial equity.

Both the efforts to extend black self-development and to influence public policy and programming must be informed by trustworthy, fact-based assessments of prevailing conditions--to support prudent prioritizing, planning, and decision-making on resource allocation. Reliable data and insightful data analysis are more critical now than ever, and there is every indication that their importance in coming years will continue to grow.

Accordingly, this report provides a comprehensive statistical examination of contemporary Black America. Although it does not come close to exhausting the critical indicators of status and progress that might be reviewed, the report includes a diversity of useful information.

Making liberal use of graphics, the report is organized in seven major sections. Section I describes the **demographic characteristics** of the black population, including population distribution, family composition, and selected vital statistics. Section II focuses on **health status** and **health care**. Section III is devoted to **education** variables, given the burgeoning importance of educational achievement in our society. Section IV covers various dimensions of **economic status**, including income, employment, earnings, occupation, and business development. Section V addresses **political empowerment**. Section VI offers some supplementary data on **black youth**. Finally, Section VII makes a few concluding observations on the overall significance and **implications** of the data.

Each data section is prefaced by a brief focusing statement. Also, each section contains concise highlight statements which summarize the statistical presentation. These features distinguish *The Black Report* from similar statistical reference works that are available. That is, existing publications do not provide much substantive context, interpretive commentary, or analytic narrative to support and embellish the statistics. *The Black Report* was designed to minimize such shortcomings. Finally, for reference purposes, black/white comparisons are standard throughout.

SECTION I

BLACK DEMOGRAPHICS

The demographics of the black population have changed markedly over the years. Most notably, blacks have become an increasingly larger proportion of the total American population, as their growth rate has exceeded that of white Americans. The significance of this fact cannot be overemphasized, as it has had broad-ranging implications in many areas. For example, growth of the black population has increased the collective economic and political power of the group in the larger society. It has also boosted the potential for self-development initiatives.

On the other hand, the pattern of growth has also brought some unwelcome consequences. Some of these are associated with the rise in out-of-wedlock births and the resultant proliferation of female-headed households. As we will see, a disproportionate number of African-American children are reared by single females. Moreover, many of these mothers are teenagers and young adults who not only lack parenting skills but also the education and training necessary to be economically self-sufficient. Thus, their children tend not to receive the guidance, support, and resources they need to develop into well-rounded, productive adults. Absent positive social intervention, these children are, from the moment they are born, virtually predestined to failure and misery in today's complex society. Indeed, children having children is one of the most serious, far-reaching problems facing Black America.

In any event, the contemporary demography of Black America needs careful understanding. It continues to change in significant ways. Just as the nation as a whole has experienced a *"demographic revolution,"* Black America has seen a corresponding revolution among its own population. Hence, any needs assessment, policy development, or programmatic undertaking--by blacks themselves or public or private agencies that would serve their interests--must be based on sound knowledge about black demographics. The data in this section are very helpful in this regard. Data are presented on population distribution, family composition,and vital statistics.

HIGHLIGHTS

- Black Americans comprise about 13 percent of the total U.S. population. This proportion is projected to reach 14 percent by the year 2020.

- Black Americans continue to be heavily concentrated in the South. An overwhelming proportion (87 percent) reside in metropolitan areas, with more than half of these living inside central cities.

- Black Americans are much more likely than whites to be single and never married. Similarly, 53 percent of black children live with their mothers only, compared to just 18 percent of white children.

- The overall black birth rate exceeds the white rate by about six percentage points, while the out-of-wedlock birth rate among blacks is three times the corresponding rate for whites.

- The black infant mortality rate is 2.5 times the rate among whites. There is also a sizable racial disparity in life expectancy-about 74 years for blacks and 80 years for whites.

Figure I.1. Total Resident Population, by Race: March 1995

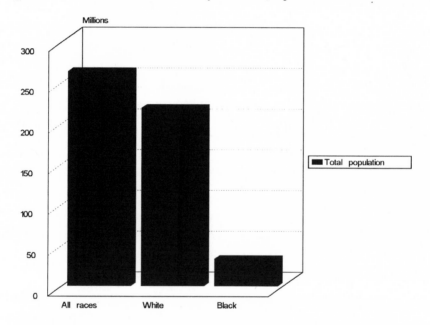

Source: U.S. Bureau of the Census, Statistical Abstract of the United States 1996, table
22, page 22

Table I.1.   U.S. Population, by Race and Sex: March 1995

(Numbers in Thousands)

Sex	All races	Black	White
Both sexes	262,755	33,141	218,085
Percent	100.0	100.0	100.0
Male	48.8	46.8	49.0
Female	51.2	53.2	51.0

Source: U.S. Census Bureau, March 1995 Current Population Survey, the Nation's African American Population, table 1

Figure I.2.   Percent Resident Population, by Race: March 1995

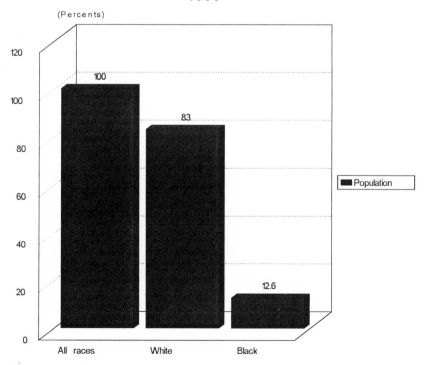

Source: U.S. Bureau of the Census, March 1995 Current Population Survey, the Nation's African American Population, table 1

Table I.2.   U.S. Population, by Race and Sex: March 1995

(Numbers in thousands)

Sex	All races	Black	White
Both sexes	262,105	33,531	192,771
Male	128,072	15,687	94,438
Female	134,033	17,844	98,334

Source: U.S. Bureau of the Census, March 1995 Current Population Survey, the Nation's African American Population, table 1

Figure IV.3.   Median Weekly Earnings of Full-Time Wage and Salary Workers by Race and Sex: 1995

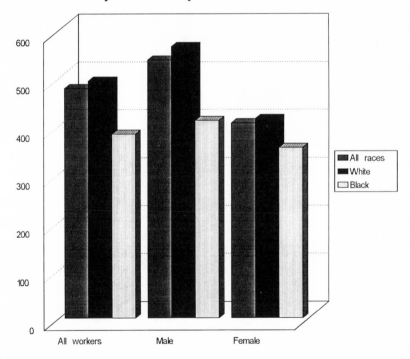

Source: U.S. Bureau of the Census, Statistical Abstract of the United States 1996, table 663, page 426

Figure I.4. Projection of the Population, By Race: Year 2020

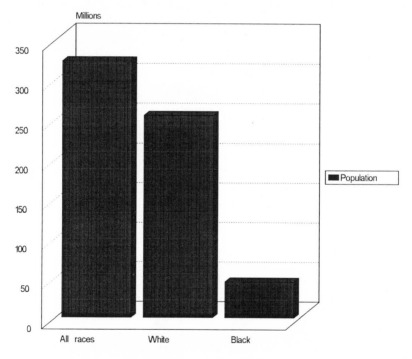

Source: U.S. Census Bureau, Current Population Reports, P25-1130. Population
Projections of the United States by Age, Race, Sex, and Hispanic Origin: 1995 to 2050.
table 2, page 76

Table I.3. Projection of the Population, by Race and Sex: Year 2020
(Numbers in thousands)

Sex	All races	Black	White
Total	325,942	45,408	254,791
Male	159,897	21,479	125,933
Female	166,045	23,929	128,858

Source: U.S. Bureau of the Census, Current Population Reports, P-25-1111, Population Projections for States, by Age, Sex, Race, and Hispanic Origin: 1993 to 2020, table 3, page 23

Figure I.5. Projection of the Population, by Race and Sex: Year 2020

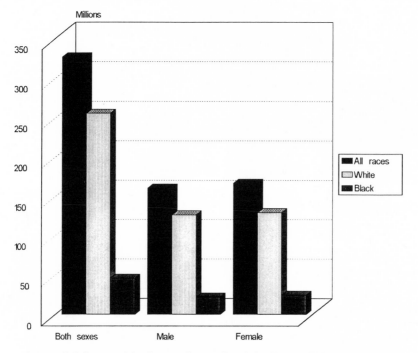

Source: U.S. Bureau of the Census, Current Population Report, P25-1111, Population Projections for States, by Age, Sex, Race, and Hispanic Origin: 1993 to 2020, table 3, page 23

Table I.4. U.S. Population, by Race and Age: March 1995
(Numbers in thousands)

Age	Total	Black	White
All Ages	262,105	33,531	192,771
Under 5 years	20,182	3,353	13,108
5-14 years	39,054	6,236	26,216
15-19 years	18,085	2,850	12,337
20-24 years	18,085	2,615	12,337
25-34 years	41,413	5,466	29,301
35-44 years	42,461	5,197	31,807
45-64 years	51,372	5,263	40,867
65-74 years	18,085	1,542	15,422
75 years & older	13,105	1,006	11,373

Source: U.S. Bureau of the Census, March 1995 Current Population Survey, the Nation's African American Population, table 1

Figure I.6. U.S. Population, by Race and Age: 1995

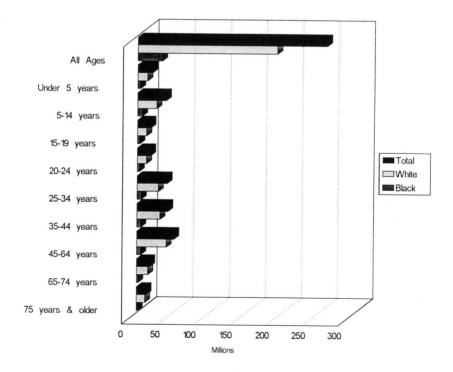

Source: U. S. Bureau of the Census, March 1995 Current Population Survey, the Nation's African American Population, table 1

Table I.5. Projection of the Population, by Race and Age: Year 2020

(Numbers in thousands)

Age	Total	Black	White
All Ages	322,742	45,075	254,887
Under 5 years	21,979	3,818	16,419
5-15 years	47,112	8,127	35,100
16-19 years	17,133	2,906	12,827
20-24 years	21,298	3,399	16,186
25-34 years	42,934	6,368	33,118
35-44 years	39,612	5,915	30,937
45-64 years	79,453	9,923	64,588
65-74 years	31,385	3,255	26,617
75 years & older	21,835	1,725	16,395

Source: U.S. Bureau of the Census, Current Population Reports, P25-1130, Population Projections of the United States by Age, Sex, Race, and Hispanic Origin: 1995 to 2050, table 2, page 76

Figure I.7. Projection of the Population, by Race and Age: Year 2020

(Numbers in thousands)

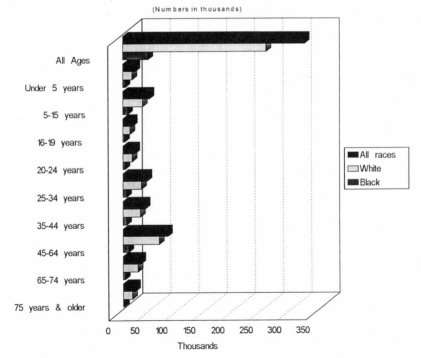

Source: U.S. Census Bureau, Current Population Reports, P25-1130, Population Projections of the United States by Age, Sex, Race. and Hispanic Origin: 1995 to 2050, table 2, page 76

Table I.6. Population Distribution, by Race and Region:
March 1995
(Numbers in thousands)

Regions	All Races	Black	White
Northeast	51,270	5,778	40,559
Midwest	61,494	6,352	52,433
South	91,896	18,613	62,645
West	57,444	2,787	37,135

Source: U.S. Census Bureau, March 1995 Current Population Survey, the Nation's
African American Population, table 3

Fiqure I.8.   Population Distribution, by Region and Race:
March 1995

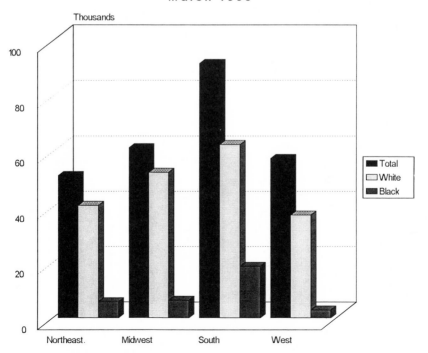

Source: U.S. Bureau of the Census, March 1995 Current Population Survey, the
Nation's African American Population, table 3

Table I.7.   Projected Population Distribution, by Race and
Region: Year 2020
(Numbers in thousands)

Region	Total	Black	White
Northeast	55,352	8,041	43,843
Midwest	68,984	8,448	57,551
South	117,498	24,074	88,736
West	84,109	4,845	64,662

Source: U.S. Bureau of the Census, Current Population Report, P25-1111, Population
Projections for States, by Age, Sex, Race, and Hispanic Origin: 1993 to 2020, table.3,
page 23.

Figure I.9.   Projected Population Distribution, by Region and
Race: Year 2020

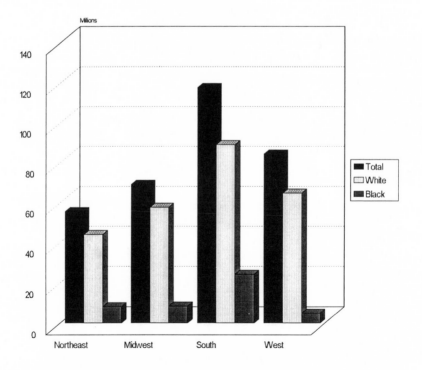

Source: U.S. Bureau of the Census, Current Population Report, P25-1111, Population
Projections for States, by Age. Sex, Race, and Hispanic Origin: 1993 to 2020, table 3.
page 23

Table I.8. Distribution of the Population, by Residence and Race: March 1995

(Numbers in thousands)

Residence	All races	Black	White
Total persons	262,105	33,531	192,771
Percent	100.0	100.0	100.0
Metropolitan areas	79.8	86.7	76.6
Inside central cities	29.5	54.9	22.4
Outside central cities	50.3	31.7	54.2
Nonmetropolitan areas	20.2	13.3	23.4

Source: U.S. Bureau of the Census, March 1995 Current Population Survey, the Nation's African American Population, table 3

Figure I.10. Distribution of the Population, by Residence and Race: March 1995

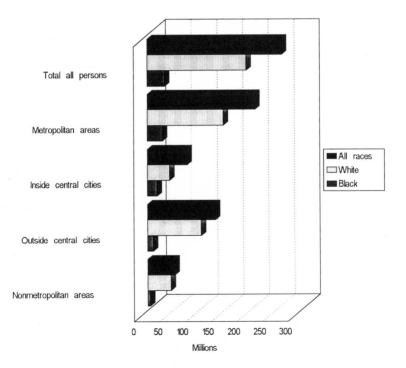

Source: U.S. Bureau of the Census. March 1995 Current Population Survey, the Nation's African American Population, table 3

Table I.9. Marital Status of the Population, by Race: March 1995

(Numbers in thousands except percents)

Marital Status	All races	Black	White
Total persons 15 years and over	202,732	23,922	153,490
Percent	100.0	100.0	100.0
Never married	27.1	43.0	23.7
Married, spouse present	54.2	32.6	58.2
Married, spouse absent	3.4	7.4	2.3
Widowed	6.6	7.1	6.9
Divorced	8.7	9.9	8.8

Source: U.S. Bureau of the Census, Current Population Survey March 1995, PPL-45, table 1

Table I.10. Family Size, by Race and Total Number of Related Children: 1995

(Numbers in thousands)

Size of Family	Total	Black	White
Total	69,313	8,093	53,024
Two persons	29,181	2,841	24,179
Three persons	15,904	2,153	11,877
Four persons	14,625	1,635	10,923
Five persons	6,284	866	4,295
Six persons	2,106	340	1,220
Seven or more persons	1,213	259	530

Source: U.S. Bureau of the Census, March 1995 Current Population Survey, the Nation's African American Population, table 6

Figure I.11. Family Size, by Race and Total Number of Related Children: 1995

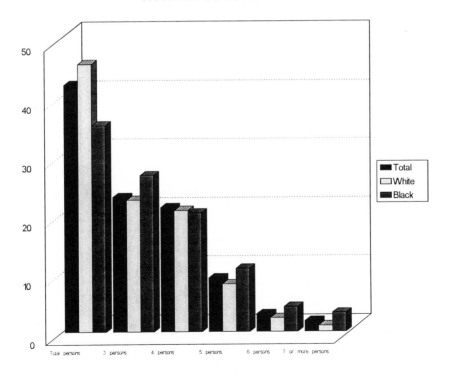

Source: U.S. Bureau of the Census, March 1995 Current Population Survey, The Nation's African American Population, table 6

Table I.11.   Living Arrangements of Children Under 18 Years Old, by Race: 1995

(Numbers in thousands except percents)

Status	Both races	Black	White
Total under 18 years old	70,254	11,301	55,327
Percent	100.0	100.0	100.0
Both parents	69	33	76
Mother only	23	52	18
Father only	4	4	3
Neither parent	4.0	11	3

Source: U.S. Bureau of the Census, Statistical Abstract of the United States 1996, table 81, page 65

Figure I.12.   Living Arrangements of Children Under 18 Years, by Race: 1995

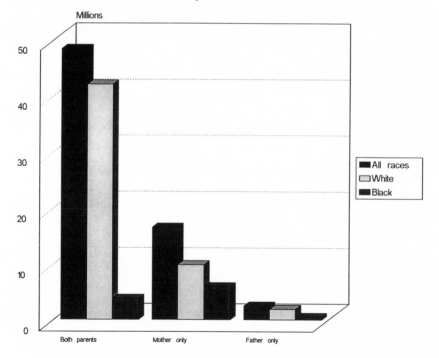

Source: U.S. Census Bureau, Statistical Abstract of the United States 1996, table 82, page 66

Table I.12. Births and Birth Rates, by Race: 1993

(Births in thousands)

Race	Births	Birth Rates
Total	4,000	15.5%
White	3,150	14.7%
Black	659	20.5%

Source: U.S. Bureau of the Census, Statistical Abstract of the United States, 1996, table 92, page 75

Figure I.13   Birth Rates, by Race: 1993

(Birth rate per 1,000 population)

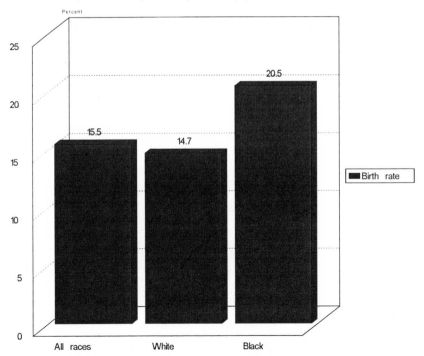

Source: U.S. Bureau of the Census, Statistical Abstract of the United States, 1996, table 92, page 75

Table I.13. Out-of-Wedlock Birth Rate, by Race of Child 1993

(Numbers in thousands, except percents)

Race of Child	Total Live Births	Percent
All races	1,240	31.0
White	742	23.6
Black	452	68.7

U.S. Bureau of the Census, Statistical Abstract of the United States 1996, table 98, page 79

Figure I.14.   Out-of-Wedlock Birth Rate, by Race of Child: 1993

(Rate per 1,000 unmarried women)

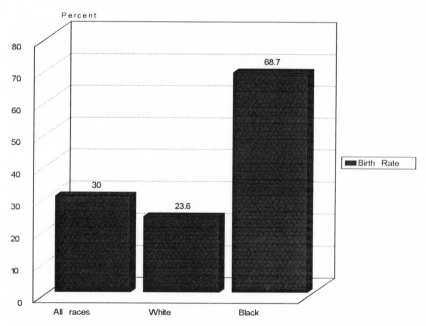

Source: U.S. Bureau of the Census, Statistical Abstract of the United States, 1996, table 98, page 79

Table I.14. Number of Deaths and Death Rates, by Race: 1994

(Rates per 1,000 population)

Race	Number of Deaths	Death Rate
All races	22,886,000	8.8%
White	1,966,000	9.1%
Black	283,000	8.7%

Source: U.S. Bureau of the Census, Statistical Abstract of the United States, 1996, table 121, page 90

Table I.15.   Infant Deaths and Mortality Rates, by Race: 1993
(Deaths per 1,000 live births)

Race	Infant Deaths	Mortality Rate
All races	33,466	8.4%
Black	10,887	16.5%
White	21,497	6.8%

Source: U.S. National Center for Health Statistics, Monthly Vital Statistics Report, Vol. 44, No. 7, Supplement, February 29. 1996, table 25, page 59.

Figure I.15.   Infant Mortality Rate, by Race: 1993
(Deaths per 1,000 live births)

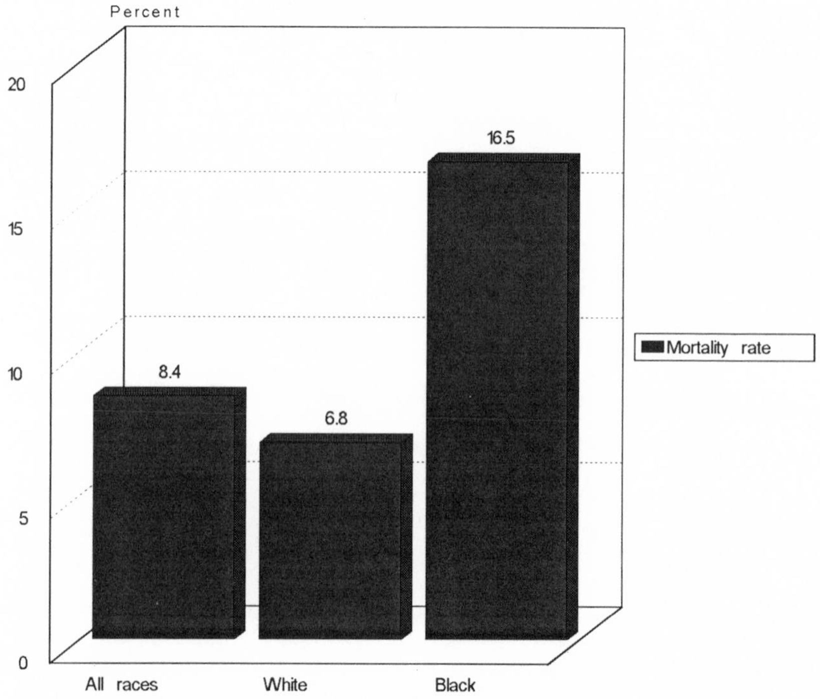

Source: U.S. Bureau of the Census, Statistical Abstract of the United States 1996, table 127, page 93

Table I.16.   Life Expectancy, by Race: 1994
(In years)

Race	Both sexes	Male	Female
All Races	75.7	72.3	79
Black	71.7	67.5	75.8
White	76.4	73.2	79.6

Source: U.S. Bureau of the Census, Statistical Abstract of the United States, 1996, table 118, page 88

Figure I.16.   Life Expectancy, by Race: 1994

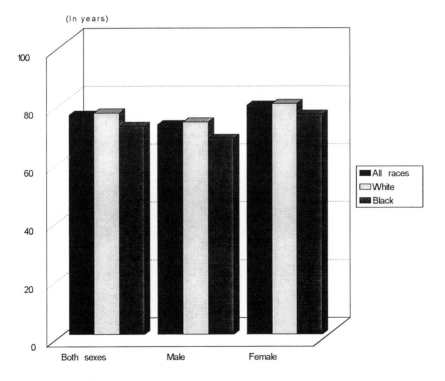

(In years)

Source: U.S. Bureau of the Census, Statistical Abstract of the United States 1996, table 118, page 88

SECTION II

BLACK HEALTH

The protracted debates over health care reform and the failure of the Clinton Administration to advance its proposals once again brought the issue of the health status of African Americans to the forefront. No other racial inequity is more consequential or longstanding than the persisting disparities in physical well-being. Likewise, pronounced differences in access to quality health care continue to divide the races. In disproportionate numbers, Black Americans lack adequate health care coverage, with equally disproportionate numbers having no insurance coverage at all. There is no question but that blacks would be prime beneficiaries of any serious reform of health care in this country.

In the meantime, the black community must press forward under the present system to enhance its health profile and cope with conditions that sometimes resemble those in developing nations. To be sure, as in other areas, the health status of blacks has improved substantially from one generation to the next. The long-term trends have been, quite literally, life-saving. However, the impressive gains are little consolation to the unacceptably large percentage of the black population beset by serious medical problems. This in a country that boasts the best medical technology and facilities in the world. This in a society where White Americans are much more likely to enjoy the benefits of good health and quality health care services.

While the Clinton Administration and the Congress failed to reach an accommodation on the question of major health care reform, the discussions were nonetheless beneficial and could be a positive omen for African Americans as well as the larger population. The fact is that public health had become a central preoccupation across the body politic well before the recent debates. Americans are generally more health conscious. The tobacco menace, the hazards of toxic waste, and the spread of HIV head a mounting list of incentives to pay more attention to our health needs and provisions for meeting them. Consequently, the issue of health care reform is sure to remain on the front burner of policy priorities, and there is good reason to expect that serious reform, of some kind, will occur in the next few years. Until then, efforts to have the present system work better, especially for groups who are in the predicament of having inordinately frequent and/or severe medical conditions but relatively limited access to quality care, should intensify.

This section describes the current health status of African Americans on selected indicators. The comparisons with whites leave no doubt that racial equity in this area must continue to be a paramount objective.

HIGHLIGHTS

- The incidence of hypertension among Black Americans--for both males and females--is significantly higher than the incidence among whites. Black females are nearly twice as likely to suffer from hypertension than are their white counterparts. Diabetes is also much more prevalent among the black population.

- Although they represent just 13 percent of the total U.S. population, Black Americans accounted for 40 percent of all reported AIDS cases in 1994, up from 32 percent in 1990.

- Only half of Black Americans are covered by private health insurance, compared to about three-fourths of the white population. Conversely, blacks are three times as likely to be insured by the government (mainly medicaid). Interestingly, about six-in-ten Black Americans below the poverty level are on medicaid, as against about four-in-ten of the white poor.

- In seeking health services, Black Americans are substantially more likely than White Americans to visit hospital emergency rooms--58 percent to 34 percent for the two groups, respectively. They are also much more likely than whites to visit for *"non-urgent"* reasons (33 vs. 18 percent).

26 THE BLACK REPORT

Table II.1. Age-Adjusted Prevalence for Selected Chronic
Health Conditions, by Race and Sex: 1986-1990

(Percent)

Condition	Black male	Black female	White male	White female
Hypertension	13.79	19.73	10.32	10.96
Asthma	4.43	5.07	4.26	4.3
Diabetes	4.13	4.89	2.45	2.36
Chronic Bronchitis	2.88	4.02	4.42	6.23
Heart disease	1.64	1.42	1.14	1.83
Stroke	1.54	1.2	1.21	0.98
Emphysema	0.93	0.17	0.26	0.58

Source: Centers for Disease Control, Chronic Disease in Minority Populations, 1994,
tables 2.5 and 2.6, pages 2-17 and 2-18

Figure II.1. Age-Adjusted Prevalence for Selected Chronic
Health Conditions, by Race and Sex: 1986-1990

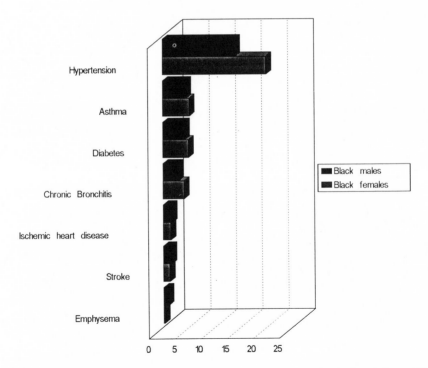

Source: Centers for Disease Control, Chronic Disease in Minority Populations, 1994,
tables 2.5 and 2.6, pages 2-17 and 2-18

Table II. 2.   Reported AIDS Cases, by Race and Year

Year	Total	Black	White
1,990	41,639	13,200	22,327
1,991	43,653	14,638	22,125
1,992	45,839	16,053	22,455
1,993	102,605	38,072	47,762
1,994	77,561	31,103	32,928
1,995	71,547	29,326	29,715
Percent			
1,990	100.0	31.7	53.6
1,991	100.0	33.5	50.7
1,992	100.0	35	49
1,993	100.0	37.1	46.5
1,994	100.0	40.1	42.5
1,995	100	41	41.5

Source: U.S. Bureau of the Census, Statistical Abstract of the United States, 1996, table 217, page 142

Figure II. 2.   Percent of Reported AIDS Cases, by Race and Year

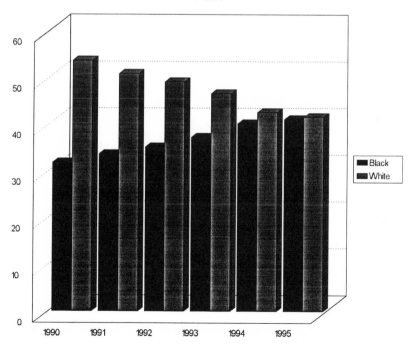

Source: U.S. Bureau of the Census, Statistical Abstract of the United States, 1996, table 217, page 142

Figure II.3. Reported AIDS Cases, by Race and Year

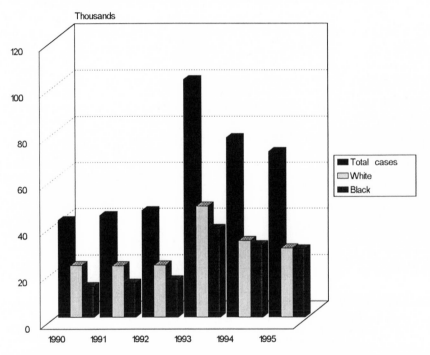

Source: U.S. Bureau of the Census, Statistical Abstract of the United States, 1996, table 217, page 142

Table II.3. Health Insurance Coverage Status, by Race and
Source of Coverage: 1995

(Percent)

Source	All races	Black	White
Total covered	84.6	79.0	85.8
Private	70.3	50.2	73.7
Government	14.3	28.8	9.6
Not covered	15.4	21.0	14.2

Source: U.S. Bureau of the Census, Current Population Reports, P60-195, September
1996, Health Insurance Coverage: 1995,

Figure II.4. Health Insurance Coverage Status, by Race and
Source of Coverage: 1995

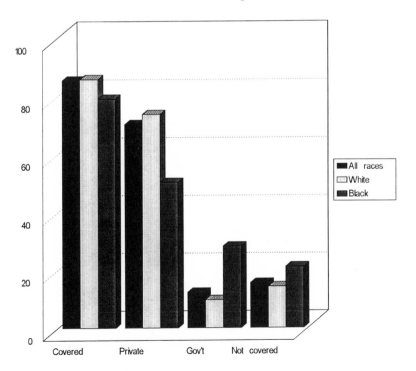

Source: U. S. Bureau of the Census, Current Population Reports, P60-195, September
1996, Health Insurance Coverage: 1995

Table II.4.   Persons Covered by Medicaid, by Race and
Poverty Status: 1994
(Numbers in thousands, except percents)

Poverty status	All races	Black	White
Total persons covered	31,401	8,896	20,347
Below poverty level	17,578	6,151	10,308
Above poverty level	13,823	2,731	10,039
Percent covered	12.0	26.7	9.4
Below poverty level	46.2	60.3	40.6
Above poverty level	6.2	11.9	5.3

Source: U.S. Bureau of the Census, Statistical Abstract of the United States, 1996,
table 169, page 118

Figure II.5. Percent of Persons Covered by Medicaid, by Race
and Poverty Status: 1994

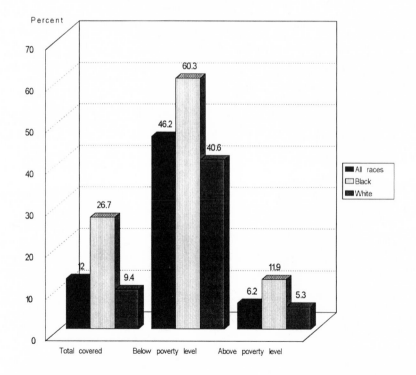

Source: U.S. Bureau of the Census, Statistical Abstract of the United States, 1996,
table 169, page 118

Table II.5. Hospital Emergency Room Visits, by Race and Condition: 1994

(Numbers in thousands, except percents)

Number of visits	All visits	Black	White
Total	93,402	18,603	72,337
Urgent	44,091	8,158	34,839
Non-urgent	49,311	10,445	37,498
Injury-related	**39,640**	**6,842**	**31,857**
Percent			
Total	36	56.3	33.7
Urgent	17	24.7	16.2
Non-urgent	19	31.6	17.5
Injury-related	15.6	20.7	14.9

Source: U.S. Bureau of the Census, Statistical Abstract of the United States, 1996, table 195, page 131

Figure II.6. Percent of Hospital Emergency Room Visits, by Race and Condition: 1994

(Visits per 100 persons)

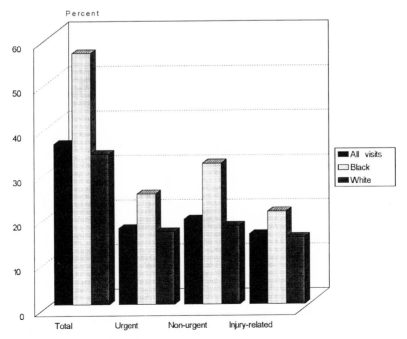

Source: U.S. Bureau of the Census, Statistical Abstract of the United States, 1996, table 195, page 131

SECTION III

BLACK EDUCATION

African Americans have always had a special appreciation for the value of education. During slavery, however, blacks were systematically denied any formal instruction or even access to instructional materials. In fact, any attempt by the slaves or their sympathizers to seek or impart learning was met by harsh penalties. And the "separate but equal" Jim Crow segregation era was maintained in a way to minimize black educational achievement. Both systems of oppression recognized that quality education was indispensable to the *"liberation"* of African Americans.

Nevertheless, the long-term progress of blacks in the education arena is impressive by any standard. For example, in 1890, only 33 percent of African-American school age children were enrolled in school. By 1970, this figure had jumped to 82 percent and is now well into the 90 percent range. No other indicator of the socioeconomic status of African Americans has posted such dramatic gains.

In contemporary times, the pivotal importance of education is uncontested. Virtually anyone, black or white, who wishes to progress and succeed in today's society, to enjoy a decent standard of living simply must possess the aptitudes and skills that education brings--and the more the better. Moreover, the demands are escalating. Transformations in the nation's economy, coupled with the irrepressible inducements of the fiercely competitive global marketplace, have raised the stakes in unprecedented ways.

There is no getting around it: education is key to economic and social well-being. Those who eschew or are disserved by the educational system are hardpressed to survive on their own, let alone flourish in their quality of life. Despite the long-term gains, all too many African Americans find themselves in this circumstance. Further, the political rhetoric stressing better education of the nation's youth in general and minority youth in particular during the past decade or so has not been matched by a commitment of resources that is commensurate with the need. Even President Clinton, who has evinced an impressive appreciation of the importance of human resource development to the nation's economic interests, thus far has not brought federal education funding levels to where they need to be. In any case, Black Americans continue to lose out. The statistics in this section illuminate this concern as well as the more positive aspects of black educational attainment.

HIGHLIGHTS

- There are persisting racial disparities in education. While the proportions of blacks and whites who have completed high school are virtually the same, blacks are much less likely to have completed four years of college (13 percent vs. 24 percent). Also, the high school dropout rate among persons 14 to 34 years old is about five percentage points higher among blacks.

- Black Americans are almost as likely as whites to be enrolled in college. For example, in the 18-4-year-old age group, the respective proportions are 56 and 58 percent. Just over 50 percent of black high school graduates go on to enroll in college, compared to 64 percent of their white counterparts.

Table. III.1. Educational Attainment, by Race: March 1995

(Persons 25 years and over)

Educational Attainment	All Races	Black	White
Total 25 years old & over	166,438	18,457	141,113
Percent			
Less than high school	18.3	26.2	17
High school graduate	33.9	36.2	34.0
1-3 years college, no degree	17.6	18.0	17.7
Associate Degree	7.1	6.3	7.3
4 or more years college	23.0	13.2	24.0

Source: U.S. Bureau of the Census, Statistical Abstract of the United States 1996, table 243, page 160

Figure. III.1. Educational Attainment, by Race: 1995

(Persons 25 years and over)

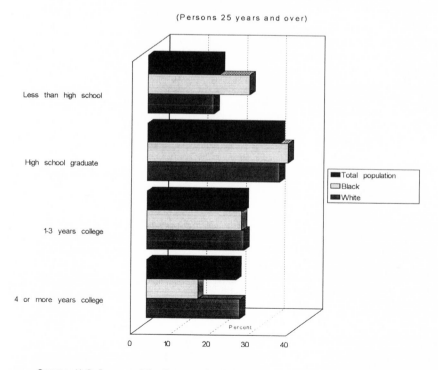

Source: U.S. Bureau of the Census, Statistical Abstract of the United States 1996, table 243, page 160

Table. III.2.   High School Dropout Rate, by Race and Sex: October 1994

Sex	All races	Black	White
Total	13.3	15.5	12.7
Male	10.3	17.5	13.6
Female	12.2	13.7	11.7

Source: U.S. Bureau of the Census, Statistical Abstract of the United States 1996, table 270, page 175

Figure. III.2.   High School Dropout Rate, by Race: 1994

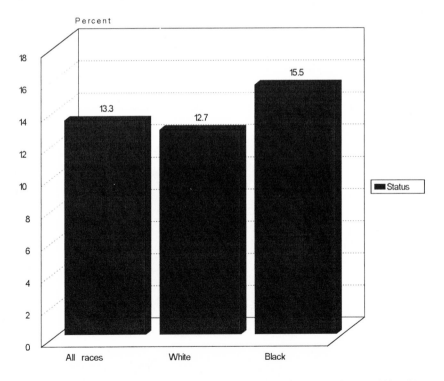

Source: U.S. Bureau of the Census, Statistical Abstract of the United States 1996, table 270, page 175

THE BLACK REPORT

Table. III.3. College Enrollment: Number of Persons 14 Years and Over Attending College, by Race: October 1994
(In thousands)

Age	All races	White	Black
Total 15 & over	15,022	12,222	1,800
15 to 17 years old	150	101	36
18 to 24 years old	8,729	7,118	1,001
25 to 34 years old	3,419	2,735	440
35 years & over	2,725	2,267	323

Source: U.S. Bureau of the Census, Current Population Survey, March 1995, Public Education Data, table 13

Figure. III.3.   College Enrollment: Number of Persons 14 Years Old and Over Attending College, by Race and Age Distribution: October 1994

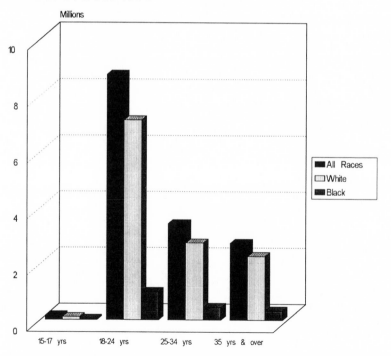

Source: U.S. Bureau of the Census, Current Population Survey, March 1996, Public Education Data, table 13

Table III.4. College Enrollment: Percent of Persons 14 Years Old and Over Attending College, by Race and Age: October 1994

(Numbers in thousands except percents)

Age	All races	White	Black
Total 15 yrs & over	15,022	12,222	1,800
Percent			
15-17 yrs	10.0	0.83	2.0
18-24 yrs	58.1	58.2	55.6
25-34 yrs	22.8	22.4	24.4
35 yrs & over	18.1	18.5	17.9

Source: U.S. Bureau of the Census, Current Population Survey, March 1996, Public Education Data, table 13

Figure. III.4.   College Enrollment: Percent of Persons 14
Years Old and Over Attending College, by Race and Age,
October 1994

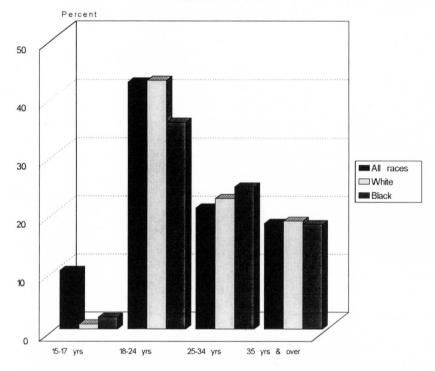

(Source: U.S. Bureau of the Census, Current Population Survey, March 1996, Public
Education Data, table 3

Table. III.5. College Enrollment: Percent High School Graduates Enrolled in College, by Race: October 1994

(Numbers in thousands, except percent)

Status	Total	White	Black
High school graduates	8,835	7,185	1,034
Percent enrolled in college	61.9	63.2	50.9

(For persons ages 16 to 24 who graduated from high school in the preceeding 12 months. Includes persons receiving GEDs. Source: U.S. Bureau of the Census, Statistical Abstract of the United States 1996, table 279, page 180

Figure. III.5. College Enrollment: Percent of High School Graduates 16 to 24 Years Old Enrolled in College, by Race: October 1994

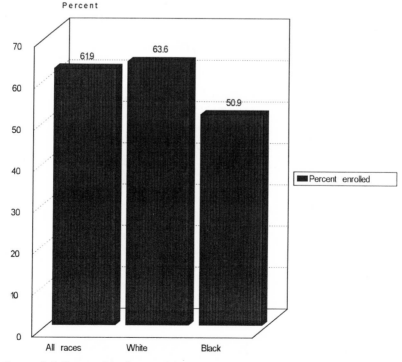

Source: U.S. Bureau of the Census, Statistical Abstract of the United States 1996, table 279, page 180

Figure. III.6.   College Enrollment: Number of High School
Graduates 16-24 Years Old Enrolled in College, by Race:
October 1994

(Numbers in thousands)

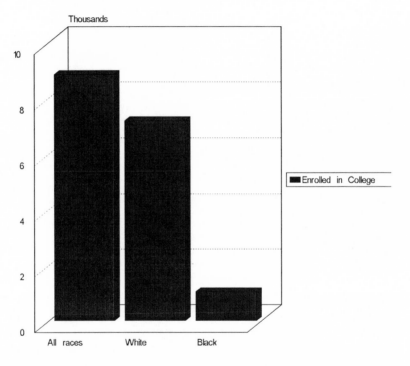

Source: U.S. Bureau of the Census, Current Population Reports, P20-487, October
1994, table 14, pages 55-57

SECTION IV

BLACK ECONOMICS

Black Americans never got their "40 acres and a mule." Instead, segregation relegated them to the fringes of the nation's economy and systematically deprived them of opportunities to advance themselves. Now, one hundred years after the "separate but equal" doctrine appeared, the economic status of blacks is vastly improved. Given the point from which they started, the change has been little short of revolutionary. Even during the 55-year-period between 1940 and 1995, for instance, blacks closed the per capita income gap with whites by almost 20 percentage points. Moreover, the economic progress of African Americans has come about largely through their own perseverance and resourcefulness, against deep-rooted institutional forces dedicated to their continued subordination. Individually and collectively, blacks, throughout their tortured history, have exercised uncommon ingenuity, resourcefulness, and adaptability in coping with economic deprivations. The historical record is replete with accounts of black advancement against the odds.

On the other hand, as we approach the year 2000, African Americans as a group are still precariously close to the edge of economic well-being. Further, they confront a public mood that has become less compassionate and supportive. Conservative sentiment posits that the nation's constitutional obligations have long since been met and that any further measures on behalf of equal economic opportunity are unnecessary. As we mentioned in the introduction, the effort to undermine affirmative action is a compelling case in point. However, the widening perception that all is well or that economic equity is a problem for blacks alone to solve disregards some harsh realities about contemporary black economic life.

To be sure, the 40-acre-and-a-mule provision (or some similar formula) would have markedly reduced the economic inequality between the races at a strategic point in the black experience. Even without this stake, however, the economic status of African Americans would look far different today had the group not been systematically hindered by ongoing discrimination in employment, business ownership, wealth accumulation, etc. Moreover, there is little question that the effects of past discriminatory practices persist as impediments to progress. This factor, coupled with the more insidious problem of institutional racism, belies the proposition that equal economic opportunity has been achieved.

This section offers a detailed examination of black economics. Data are presented on income, employment, earnings, occupation, poverty, business development, and consumer spending. The bottom line is undeniable: Economic equity remains a far distant goal.

HIGHLIGHTS

- The per capita income of Black Americans is only 60 percent of the per capita income of whites. The racial gap is even larger in family income, as black families average only 56 percent of the income of white families.

- The unemployment rate among the black workforce continues to be more than double the rate among white workers. There is a six percentage point difference in labor force participation rates in favor of whites. Among males, however, the disparity is 11 percentage points.

- Black workers average about 77 percent of the earnings of white workers. The relative position of black female workers is better at 85 percent, with black male workers averaging just 73 percent of the earnings of their white counterparts.

- Black workers are less likely than whites to be in high status occupations and more likely to be on the lower rungs of the occupational ladder. For example, 15 percent of whites have managerial type jobs, compared to nine percent of blacks. There is a similar disparity in professional occupations.

- The poverty rate among black families is three times the rate for white families. The racial gap for persons is somewhat lower, with blacks being 2.6 times more likely to be poor.

- Black-owned businesses account for merely 3.6 percent of all U.S. businesses. Moreover, the average gross receipts of black-owned businesses is decidedly lower than that for all businesses. Ninety percent of black businesses have no paid employees, compared to 82 percent of all businesses. Compared to the national average, Black Americans spend a disproportionate amount of their income on housing. They spend less than the average on transportation, health care, and entertainment.

Table IV.1.   Money Income of Families--Percent Distribution, by Income Levels and Race: 1995

Percent Distribution	All Families	White	Black
Under $5000	2.7	2.0	7.9
$5000-$9999	4.8	3.8	11.5
$10000-$14999	6.5	5.8	10.9
$15000-$24999	14.4	13.9	18.3
$25000-$34999	14.1	14.2	14.3
$35000-$49999	18.5	18.8	15.9
$50000-$74999	20.4	21.4	13.3
$75000-$99999	9.6	10.2	5.2
$100000 & over	9.0	9.8	2.8
Median income (dollars)	$40,611	$42,646	$25,970

Source: U.S. Bureau of the Census, Current Population Reports, P60-193, Consumer Income, table B-4, page B-10

Table IV.2.   Employment Status of the Civilian Population,
Race: May 1996

(In thousands except as indicated. Persons 16 years old and over)

Employment Status	All Workers	White	Black
Civilian population	200,278	166,098	23,549
Civilian labor force	133,558	112,854	15,080
Percent	66.7	67.1	64.0
Employed	126,391	107,536	13,571
Employment ratio	63.1	64.0	57.6
Unemployed	7,166	5,317	1,510
Unemployment rate	5.4	4.7	10.0
Not in labor force	66,721	55,244	8,469

Source: U.S. Bureau of Labor Statistics. Employment and Earnings. June 1996

Figure IV.1.   Employment Status of the Civilian Population,
by Race: May 1996

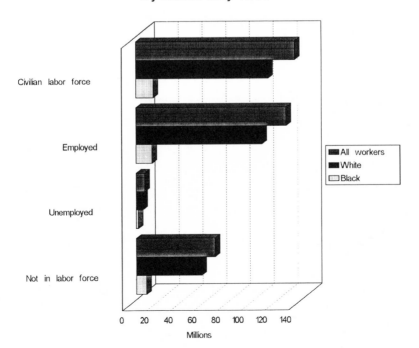

Source: U.S. Bureau of Labor Statistics, Employment and Earnings, Monthly, June 1996

Table IV.3.   Civilian Labor Force Participation Rates, by Race
and Sex: May 1996

(Percent for persons 16 years and over)

Sex	Total	White	Black
Both sexes	63.1	64.0	57.6
Men	71.1	72.4	61.5
Women	55.8	56.1	54.5

Source: U.S. Bureau of Labor Statistics, Employment and Earnings, Monthly, June 1996

Figure IV.2.   Civilian Labor Force Participation Rates, by
Race: May 1996

(persons 16 years and over)

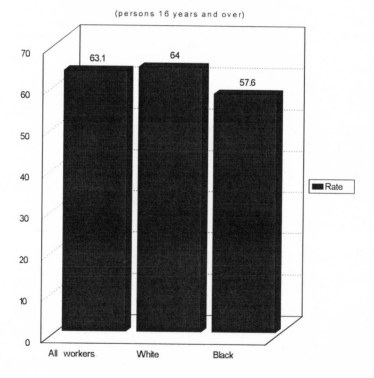

Source: U.S. Bureau of Labor Statistics, Employment and Earnings, Monthly, June 1996

Table IV.4.   Median Weekly Earnings for Full-Time Wage and
Salary Workers, by Race and Sex: 1995

Race	All Workers		Male	Female
All races	$479		$538	$406
White	$494		$566	$415
Black	$383		$411	$355

Source: U.S. Bureau of the Census, Statistical Abstract of the United States 1996, table
663, page 426

Figure IV.3.   Median Weekly Earnings of Full-Time Wage and
Salary Workers by Race and Sex: 1995

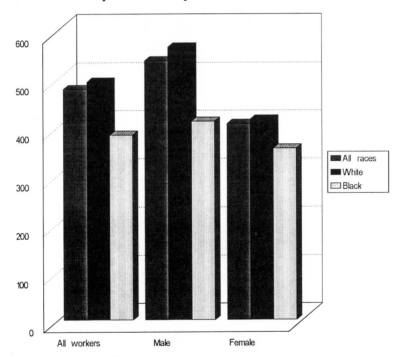

Source: U.S. Bureau of the Census, Statistical Abstract of the United States 1996, table
663, page 426

Table IV.5. Occupational Attainment, by Race: March 1996

Occupation	Total employed	White	Black
Total 16 yrs & over	124,554	106,116	13,274
Percent	**100.0**	**100.0**	**100.0**
Exec, admin, & managerial	13.6	14.4	8.9
Professional specialty	14.7	15.1	10.6
Technicians & related support	3.1	3.1	2.9
Sales occupations	12.0	12.5	8.9
Admin support including clerical	14.7	14.5	16.9
Private household	0.6	0.5	0.8
Protective service	1.8	1.7	2.9
Other services	11.3	10.3	17.9
Precision production, craft, & repair	10.8	11.2	8.0
Machine operators, assemblers, & inspectors	6.4	5.9	9.2
Transportation & material movers	4.1	4.0	6.2
Handlers, cleaners, helpers, & laborers	3.9	3.6	5.6
Farming, fishing, & forestry	3.0	3.2	1.2

Source: U.S. Bureau of Labor Statistics, Employment and Earnings June 1996

Table IV.6.   Families Below   the Poverty, by Race: 1995
(Number in thousands, except percents)

Status	All families	White	Black
Total families	69,597	58,872	8,055
Below poverty	7,532	4,994	2,127
Percent	10.8	8.5	26.4

Source: U.S. Bureau of the Census, Current Population Reports, P60-194, Poverty in the United States: 1995, table C-3, page C-11

Figure IV.4.   Percent of Families Below the Poverty Level, by Race: 1995

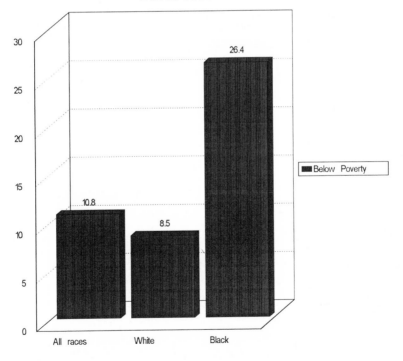

Source: U.S. Census Bureau, Current Population Reports, P60-194, Poverty in the United States: 1995. table A, page vii

Table IV.7. Persons Below the Poverty Level, by Race: 1995

(In thousands, except percents)

Race	Total	Below poverty	Percent
All races	263,733	36426	13.8
White	218,028	24423	11.2
Black	33,740	9872	29.3

Source: U.S. Bureau of the Census, Current Population Reports, P60-194, Poverty in the United States:1995, table A, page vii

Figure IV.5.   Percent of Persons Below the Poverty Level, by Race: 1995

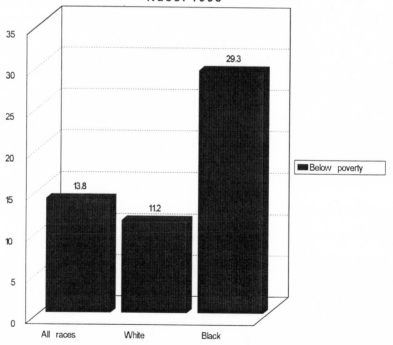

Source: U.S. Bureau of the Census, Current Population Reports, P60-194, Poverty in the United States: 1995, table A, page vii

Table IV.8. Black-Owned Businesses, by Major Industry Group: 1992

Industry Group	All Businesses	Black-Owned Businesses
Construction	1,829,620	43,381
Manufacturing	517,714	10,469
Transportation/Utilities	698,903	49,095
Wholesale trade	538,339	7,550
Retail trade	2,478,045	86,840
Finance, Insurance, Real Estate	1,941,029	40,924
Services	7,784,016	332,981
Agri/Mining	583,253	10,309
Industries not classified	882,224	39,363

2,37%

Source: U.S. Bureau of the Census, Survey, of Minority-Owned Business Enterprises, table 1, page 9

Table IV.9. Black-Owned Businesses, by Legal Form of Organization: 1992
(In thousands)

Legal Form	All Businesses	Black-Owned Businesses
All Industries	17,253	621
Sole proprietorships	14,599	584
Partnerships	1,090	15
Subchapter S Corp.	1,564	22

Source: U.S. Bureau of the Census, Survey of Minority-Owned Business Enterprises, table 7, page 69

Figure IV.6. Black-Owned Businesses, by Legal Form of Organization: 1992

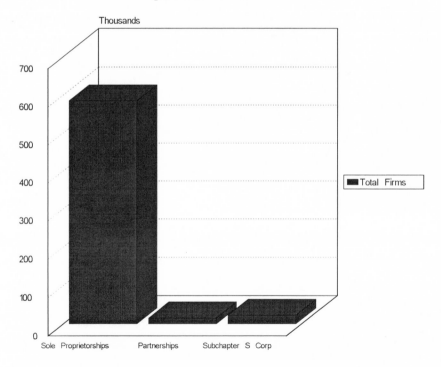

Source: U.S. Bureau of the Census, Survey of Minority-Owned Business Enterprises, table 7, page 69

Table. IV.10. Number of Black-Owned Businesses, by Annua Gross Receipt Size: 1992

Gross receipts	All Firms	Black-Owned Firms
Total	17,253,143	620,912
Less than $5,000	5,226,553	236,722
$5,000 to $9,999	2,443,946	111,512
$10,000 to $24,999	3,076,410	129,901
$25,000 to $49,999	1,945,806	62,209
$50,000 to $99,999	1,615,940	39,218
$100,000 to $249,999	1,499,790	25,469
$250,000 to $499,999	682,583	9,029
$500,000 to $999,999	372,078	3,823
$1,000,000 or more	390,037	3,028

Source: U.S. Bureau of the Census, Survey of Minority-Owned Business Enterprises, tables 7 and 13, page 69

Figure. IV.7. Nunber of Black-Owned Businesses, by Annual Gross Receipts: 1992

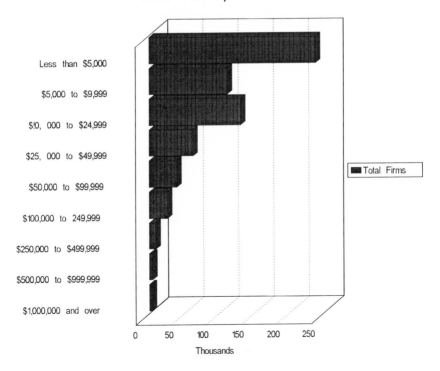

Source: U.S. Bureau of the Census, Survey of Minority-Owned Business Enterprises, table 13, page 75

Table IV.11. Percent of Black-Owned Businesses, by Annual
Gross Receipts: 1992

(In millions except as indicated)

Annual Receipts	All Businesses	Black-Owned Businesses
Total Firms	17,253,143	620,912
Total Receipts	3,324,200	32,197
Percent	100.0	100.0
Less than $5,000	30.3	38.1
$5,000 to $9,999	14.2	18.0
$10,000 to $24,999	17.8	20.9
$25,000 to $49,999	11.3	10.0
$50,000 to $99,999	9.4	6.3
$100,000 to $249,999	8.7	4.1
$250,000 to $499,999	4.0	1.5
$500,000 to $999,999	2.2	0.6
$1,000,000 or more	2.3	0.5

Source: U.S. Bureau of the Census, Survey of Minority-Owned Business Enterprise
tables 7 and 13, pages 69 and 75

Table IV.12.   Black-Owned Busineses, by Employment Size
of Firm: 1992

Employment Size	All Businesses	Black-Owned Businesses
All Industries	17,253,143	620,912
With no paid employees	14,118,184	556,434
With paid employees	3,134,959	64,478
No employees	435,838	13,725
1 to 4 employees	1,716,076	37,587
5 to 9 employees	503,808	7,853
10 to 19 employees	256,110	2,839
20 to 49 employees	144,734	1,700
50 to 99 employees	45,331	432
100 or more employees	33,062	342

Source: U.S. Bureau of the Census, Survey of Minority-Owned Business Enterprises,
table 9, page 71

Figure IV.8.   Black-Owned Businesses, by Employment Size
of Firm: 1992

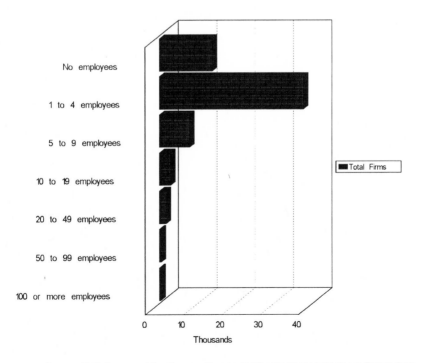

Source: U.S. Bureau of the Census, Survey of Minority-Owned Business Enterprises,
table 9, page 71

Fiqure IV.9.   Black-Owned Businesses as a Percent of all
U.S. Businesses: 1992

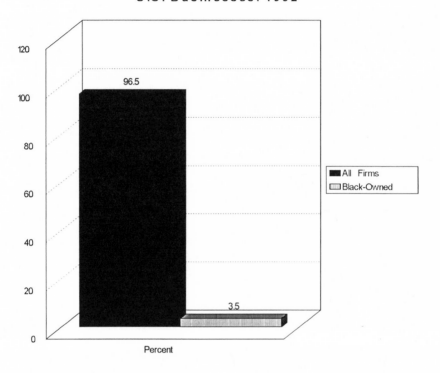

Source: U.S. Bureau of the Census, Survey of Minority-Owned Business Enterprises,
tables A and B, page 2

Table IV.13. Average Annual Expenditures on Common
Consumer Items, by Race: 1994

Item	All Consumers	White	Black
No. of Consumers (000's)	102,210	88,537	11,513
Average Annual Expenditure	**$31,751**	**$32,935**	**$22,418**
Food	$4,411	$4,552	$3,390
Alcoholic beverages	$278	$295	$149
Housing	$10,106	$10,415	$7,673
Apparel & services	$1,644	$1,651	$1,592
Transportation	$6,044	$6,268	$4,271
Health care	$1,755	$1,860	$923
Entertainment	$1,567	$1,668	$767
Personal care products & services	$397	$401	$360
Reading	$165	$176	$77
Education	$460	$485	$29
Tobacco products & smoking supplies	$259	$266	$202
Cash contributions	$960	$1,019	$494

Source: U.S. Bureau of the Census, Statistical Abstract of the United States 1996, table 704, page 457

Figure IV.10. Average Annual Expenditures on Common
Consumer Items, by Race: 1994

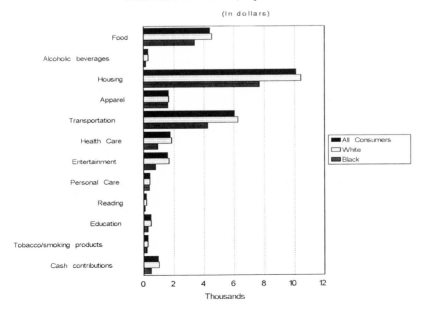

Source: U.S. Bureau of of the Census, Statistical Abstract of the United States 1996, table 704, page 457

SECTION V

BLACK POLITICAL EMPOWERMENT

Ours is a *power*-oriented society. Although it can take many forms, the reference here is to the collective power exercised by groups seeking to advance their social and economic interests within the framework of participatory democracy--i.e., political power. Thus, political power is not construed to mean well-being per se. Rather, it constitutes a means through which group well-being is pursued. Legislative provisions governing conduct of domestic affairs, decisions about the allocation of public resources, and the development of regulations according to which rewards and benefits are distributed are all outcomes of the exercise of power in the American political process.

The historical African-American experience is distinguished first and foremost by the group's limited ability to influence political outcomes favorable to its interests. It is distinguished by a condition of *powerlessness*--dependency upon the goodwill of others for one's own welfare. For a time, this condition was absolute, as African Americans were legally prohibited from participating in the formal political process. Subsequently, the disenfranchisement was effected through discriminatory applications of rules and practices regulating political participation. Thus, the life experiences of and possibilities for blacks in this country must be understood in power--i.e., political--terms.

The 1965 Voting Rights Act had a pronounced impact on black political participation and racial differences in political involvement. Most directly, the legislation facilitated the black vote, whereby African Americans were enabled to participate in the electoral process, to support candidates whom they favored. In turn, the increased voter participation expanded dramatically the number of African Americans seeking and winning political office. At the national level, this scenario is prominently symbolized by the rise of the Congressional Black Caucus, which numbered 40 members at the start of the 1995 session of Congress.

The data in this section detail the contemporary status of black political empowerment. Specifically, they focus on the two basic forms of political participation--voting and officeholding.

HIGHLIGHTS

- Fifty-eight percent of voting age Black Americans were registered to vote in the1994 off-year elections, compared to 64 percent of whites. The corresponding figures for 1992 were 64 percent and 70 percent.

- Only 37 percent of registered blacks actually voted in 1994, down considerably from 54 percent in 1992. Although whites were much more likely to vote in both instances, they also exhibited lower turnout in 1994 than in 1992.

- Even among the 18-24-year-old college student population, blacks were less likely to register and vote than whites. The racial disparities were narrower among persons not in college.

- Black adults are far more likely than their white counterparts to identify with the Democratic Party. They are also more likely to classify themselves as Independent.

- Black Americans account for just 2.4 percent of all local elected officials in the country. Their representation is highest among school district officials (4.9 percent).

Table. V.1. Registration and Voting of Voting Age Population, by Race: 1992 and 1994

Status	Total	Black	White
1994			
Voting age pop	190.3 million	21.3 million	160.3 million
Registered	62.0%	58.3%	64.2%
Voting	44.6%	37.0%	46.9%
1992			
Voting age pop	185.7 million	21.0 million	157.8 million
Registered	68.2%	63.9%	70.1%
Voting	61.3%	54.0%	63.6%

Source: U.S. Bureau of the Census, Statistical Abstract of the United States, 1995, table 459, page 289

Figure. V.1. Percent of Blacks of Voting Age Registering and Voting: 1992 and 1994

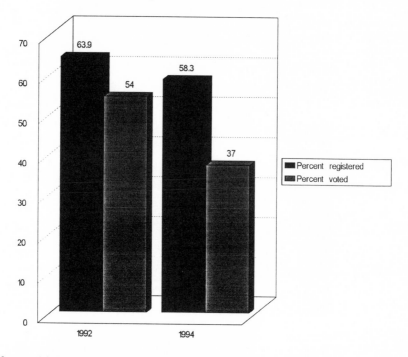

Source: U.S. Bureau of the Census, Statistical Abstract of the United States, 1995, Table 459, p. 289.

Table. V.2. Percent of Persons 18-24 Years Old Reporting Having Registered or Voted, by Race and College Enrollment Status: November 1994

Status	Total	Black	White
Registered			
Total 18-24 years	42.3	41.9	43.9
In college	54.9	50.4	58.2
Not in college	36.7	40.3	37.1
Voted			
Total 18-24 years	20.1	17.4	21.1
In college	26.9	23.6	28.5
Not in college	16.7	15.5	17.5

Source: U S. Bureau of the Census, "Highlights From the November 1994 Voting Survey"

Figure. V.2.   Percent of Blacks 18-24 Years Old Reporting Having Registered or Voted, by College Enrollment Status: November 1994

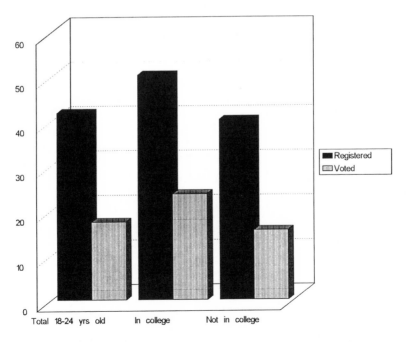

Source: U S. Bureau of the Census, "Highlights from the November 1994 Voting Survey"

Table. V.3. Political Party Identification of Adult Population, by Race and Degree of Attachment: 1994

Political party identification	Black	White
Strong Democrat	38.0	12.0
Weak Democrat	23.0	19.0
Independent Democrat	20.0	12.0
Independent	8.0	10.0
Independent Republican	4.0	13.0
Weak Republican	2.0	16.0
Strong Republican	3.0	17.0
Apolitical	1.0	1.0

Source: U.S. Bureau of the Census, Statistical Abstract of the United States, 1995, table 458, page 288

Figure. V.3. Political Party Identification of Adult Population, by Race and Degree of Attachment: 1994

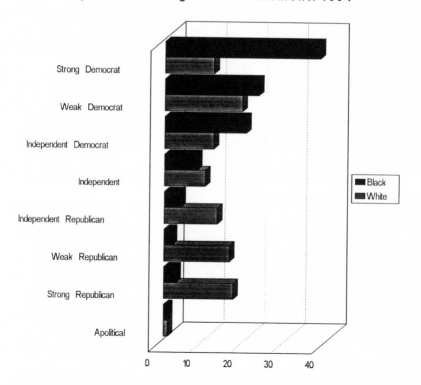

Source: U.S. Bureau of the Census, Statistical Abstract of the United States, 1995, table 458, page 288

Table. V.4.   Local Elected Officials, by Race and Type of Government: 1992

Type of government	Total	Black	White
Total	493,830	11,542	405,905
County	58,818	1,715	52,705
Municipal	135,531	4,566	114,880
Town/Township	126,958	369	102,676
School District	88,434	4,222	73,894
Special District	84,089	670	61,750

Source: U.S. Bureau of the Census, Statistical Abstract of the United States 1996, table 450, page 283

Figure. V.4.   Percent Local Elected Officials, by Race and Type of Government: 1992

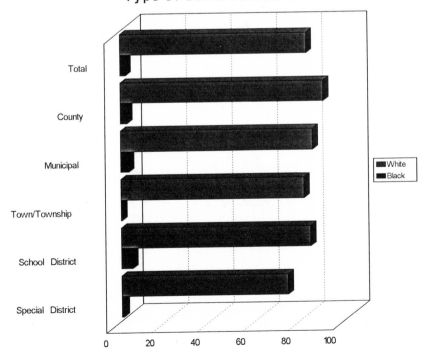

Source: U.S. Bureau of the Census, Census of Governments, Popularly Elected Officials in 1992, Preliminary Report (GC92-2)

Table. V.5.   Percent of Local Elected Officials, by Race and
Type of Government: 1992

Type of government	Black	White
Total	2.3	82.2
County	2.9	89.6
Municipal	3.4	84.8
Town/Township	0.3	80.9
School District	4.8	83.6
Special District	0.8	73.4

Source: U.S. Bureau of the Census, Statistical Abstract of the United States 1996, table
450, page 283

SECTION VI

BLACK YOUTH

Both the promise and the peril of African Americans are inextricably tied to the condition of black youth--the younger generation. In recent years, however, the promise has been diluted by an assortment of social problems. Some have external causes, while others emanate largely from within the black community itself. The latter point is poignantly illustrated by the previously mentioned problem of black youth violence. At the extreme, black male youth continue to kill one another at an alarming rate. Equally distressing is the recent sharp increase in the rate of suicide among young black males. These circumstances alone have grave implications for the future of the black community.

A prime example of the external causes of what might legitimately be called the crisis of black youth is the undereducation they frequently experience. In many urban areas, the educational system for the primary and secondary grades has been a dismal failure in affording black students the academic preparation they need to succeed in our credentials-oriented, skills-demanding society. The institutional pushout phenomenon is alive and well, as is the race-based practice of unjustifiably labeling black children slow or retarded and relegating them to the backwaters of educational achievement.

These are just two examples of degeneration that command concern. There are many more. Consequently, the black community is challenged as never before to promote more wholesome social and cultural development among its children.

Of course, the situation is not totally bleak. To the contrary, untold numbers of black youth are excelling academically and behaving in eminently responsible, productive ways. They are a genuine source of pride and reassurance to the adult generation. Unfortunately, however, the success stories have become le compelling than the failures. The promise is yielding to the perils. In this regard, one might be encouraged by the fact that both the national leadership and a growing number of public interest groups have adopted "saving the children" as the country's preeminent mission and mandate. There is a deepening realization that the entire society and its position in the world community are at risk. Continued neglect of the younger generation is nothing short of a recipe for national disaster.

Just how well these expressions of concern translate into beneficial policies and programs, however, remains to be seen. The black community and its youth have a special interest in the outcomes. The supplementary data in this section speak to these issues.

HIGHLIGHTS

• Unemployment among black teenagers is 2.3 times the rate for white teens. The racial unemployment gap among female teens is somewhat wider at 2.4 to1.

• Black teenagers age 15-19 years have a birth rate of 118.9 per 1000, compared to a 43.4 per 1000 rate for their white counterparts.

• Forty-two percent of black children live in poverty, 26 percent more than white children (16 percent).

• Young blacks (i.e., 24 years and below) are much more likely to die from homicide/legal intervention than their white counterparts.

• Black juveniles account for a greatly disproportionate number of all juvenile homicide offenders (62 percent), and their representation has grown dramatically during the past decade, having stood at 45 percent in 1984.

• Blacks are also overrepresented among juvenile homicide *victims*, making up 52 percent of the total in 1994. Likewise, black juvenile homicide victims are killed predominantly by firearms. Seventy-one percent died from this cause in 1994, up from 41 percent in 1984. The corresponding figures for white victims are 56 and 38 percent.

• Blacks account for 29 percent of all juvenile arrests and an astounding50 percent of arrests for violent crimes.

• About four-in-ten black teenagers (16-19 years) neither attend school nor work, as against less than two-in-ten white teens.

Table. VI.1.   Children Under 18 Years Old Below the Poverty
Level, by Race: 1995
(Number in thousands)

Status	All races	Black	White
Total children	70,566	11,369	55,444
No. below poverty	14,665	4,761	8,981
Percent below poverty	20.8	41.9	16.2

Source: U.S. Bureau of the Census, Current Population Reports, P60-194, Poverty in
the United States: 1995, table C-2, page C-5

Figure. VI.1.   Percent of Children 18 Years and Under Below
the Poverty Level, by Race: 1995

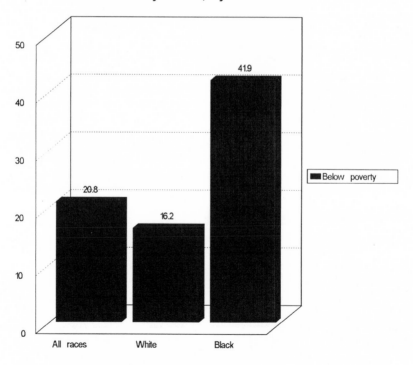

Source: U.S. Bureau of the Census, Current Population Reports, P60-194, Poverty in
the United States: 1995, table C-2, page C-5

Table. VI.2.   Health Insurance Status for Persons Under 18
Years, by Race and Source of Coverage: 1995
(Numbers in thousands, except percents)

Source	All races	Black	White
Total Covered	71,146	11,518	55,858
Percent	86.2	84.7	86.6
Private	66.1	43.9	71
Government	26.4	48.8	21.2
Not covered	13.8	15.3	13.4

Source: U.S. Bureau of the Census, Current Population Survey March 1996, Current
Population Reports, P60-195, table 1

Figure. VI.2.   Health Insurance Coverage Status for Persons
Under 18 Years, by Race and Source of Coverage: 1995

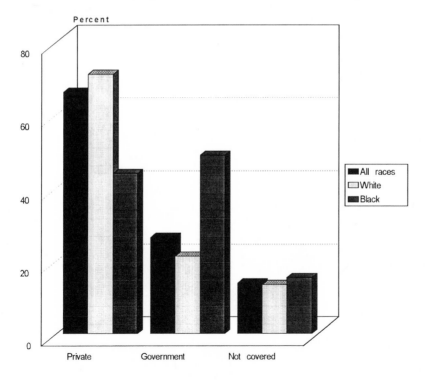

Source: U.S. Bureau of the Census, Current Population Survey, March 1996, Current
Population Reports, P60-195, table 1

Table. VI.3. Deaths, by Race and Selected Causes, 24 Years and Younger: 1993

Cause of death	All races	Black	White
Heart disease	2,300	700	1,400
Cancer	3,400	600	2,800
Accidents	21,000	3,700	16,500
Cerebrovascular diseases	500	Z*	500
Chronic obstructive pulmonary diseases	500	200	200
Pneumonia	1,100	400	700
Suicide	5,100	600	4,300
Chronic liver disease, cirrhosis	Z*	Z*	Z*
Diabetes mellitus	100	Z*	100
Homicide/legal intervention	9,900	5,700	3,800

Source: U.S. Bureau of the Census, Statistical Abstract of the United States 1996, table 130, page 95; * Z is fewer than 50 cases

Table. VI.4.   Violent Deaths, by Race and Cause, 24 Years and Younger: 1993

Cause of death	All races	Black	White
Total violent deaths	147,600	27,900	115,500
Accidents	21,000	3,700	16,500
Percent	14.2	13.3	14.3
Suicides	5,100	600	4,300
Percent	3.5	2.2	3.7
Homicides	9,900	5,700	3,800
Percent	6.7	20.4	3.3

Source: U.S. Bureau of the Census, Statistical Abstract of the United States 1996, table 130, page 95

Figure. VI.4.   Percent of Juvenile Homicide Offenders, by Race: 1984 and 1994

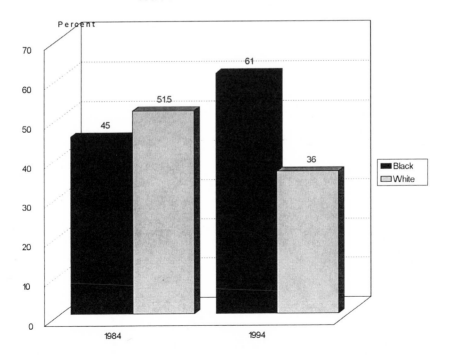

Source: Office of Juvenile Justice and Delinquency Prevention, Juvenile Offenders and Victims: 1996 Update on Violence, page 22

Figure. VI.4.   Percent of Juvenile Homicide Offenders, by Race: 1984 and 1994

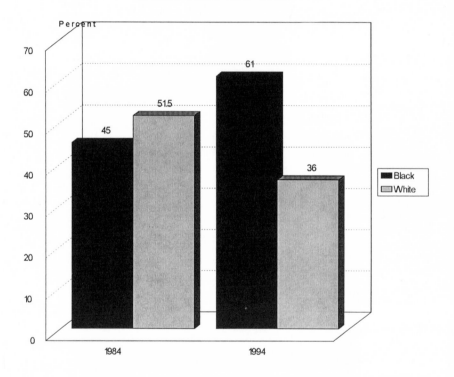

Source: Office of Juvenile Justice and Delinquency Prevention, Juvenile Offenders and Victims: 1996 Update on Violence, page 22

Figure. VI.5.   Number of Juvenile Homicide Offenders, by
Race: 1984 and 1994

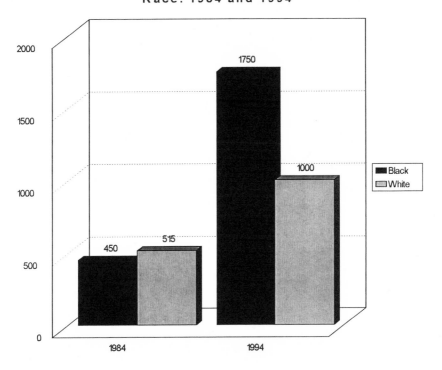

Source: Office of Juvenile Justice and Delinquency Prevention, Juvenile Offenders and
Victims: 1996 Update on Violence, page 22

Table. VI.5.   Number and Proportion of Total Juvenile Homicide
Victims, by Race: 1994

Victims	Black	White
Number	1,380	1,180
Percent	52	44

Source: Office of Juvenile Justice and Delinquency Prevention, Juvenile Offenders and
Victims: 1996 Update on Violence, page 4

Figure. VI.6.   Percent of Juvenile Homicide Victims, by Race:
1994

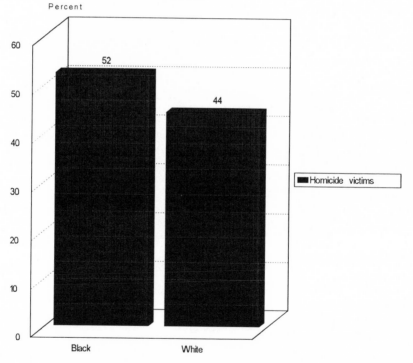

Source: Office of Juvenile Justice and Delinquency Prevention, Juvenile Offenders and
Victims: 1996 Update on Violence, page 4

Figure. VI.7. Percent of Juvenile Homicide Victims Killed by
Firearms, by Race: 1984 and 1994

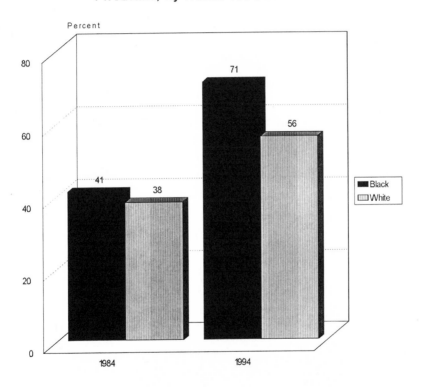

Source: Office of Juvenile Justice and Delinquency Prevention, Juvenile Offenders and
Victims: 1996 Update on Violence, page 3

THE BLACK REPORT

Table. VI.6.   Juvenile Arrests, by Race and Crime Index: 1994

Crime Index	Juvenile arrests	Black	White
Total	2,714,000	787,060	1,872,660
Percent	100.0	29.0	69.0
Crime Index Total	898,300	287,456	583,895
Percent	100.0	32.0	65.0
Violent Crime Index	150,200	75,100	72,096
Percent	100.0	50.0	48.0
Property Crime Index	748,100.0	209,468.0	516,189.0
Percent	100.0	28.0	69.0
Nonindex Offenses	1,815,700	490,239	1,270,990
Percent	100.0	27.0	70.0

Source: Office of Juvenile Justice and Delinquency Prevention, Juvenile Offenders and Victims: 1996 Update on Violence, page 10

Figure. VI.8.   Percent of Juvenile Arrests, by Race and Crime Index: 1994

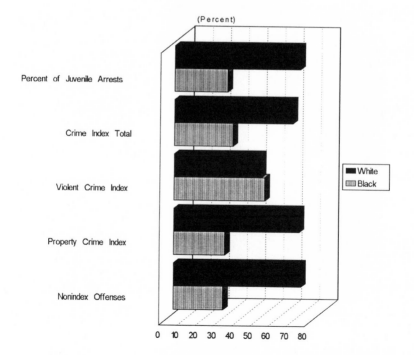

Source: Office of Juvenile Justice and Delinquency Prevention, Juvenile Offenders and Victims: 1996 Update on Violence, page 10

Table.VI.7.   Deaths by Firearms, by Race, Sex, and Selected Age Groups: 1994

Age Group	Total Black	Black male	Black female	Total White	White male	White female
All ages	11,763	10,310	1,453	26,948	22,680	4,268
5-14 years	295	223	72	508	389	119
Percent	2.5	2.1	0.69	1.9	1.7	2.8
15-24 years	5,275	4,783	492	5,625	4,896	729
Percent	44.8	46.4	33.9	20.9	21.6	17.1

Source: Centers for Disease Control and Prevention, Monthly Vital Statistics Report. Vol.44., No. 7, February 1996, table 10, page 32

Figure. VI.9.   Percent of Deaths From Firearms, for Males 15-24 Years Old, by Race: 1994

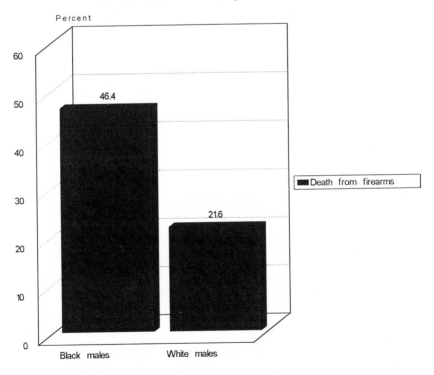

Source: Centers for Disease Control and Prevention, Monthly Vital Statistics Report, Vol. 44., No. 7, February 1996, table 10, page 32

82

THE BLACK REPORT

Table. VI.8.   Teens 16-19 Years Old Not Attending School and Not Working, by Race: May 1996

Status	Black	White
Total	595,000	2,704,000
In civilian labor force	398,000	2,052,000
Number unemployed	156,000	352,000
Percent unemployed	39.1	17.2

Source: U. S. Bureau of Labor Statistics, Employment and Earnings. June 1996, table A-15, page 46

Figure. VI.10.   Percent Teens 16-19 Years Old Not Attending School and Not Working, by Race: May 1996

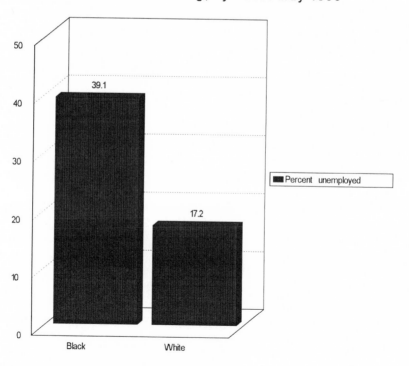

Source: U.S. Bureau of Labor Statistics, Employment and Earnings, June 1996, table A-15. page 46

SECTION VII

CONCLUDING COMMENTS

This report has provided a detailed, comprehensive statistical examination of the demographic and socioeconomic conditions of today's black population. The data are intended to further general understanding and to aid in the development of more effective public policies and private initiatives on behalf of African-American advancement and well-being at this critical juncture in the group's history. The report should be a valued reference work for these purposes.

Unsurprisingly, the statistical data paint a mixed picture of contemporary Black America. Some indicators of well-being are reasonably gratifying to observe. These positives must be appreciated for what they are--successful outcomes of the relentless, painful struggle against systematized oppression; affirmations of the efficacy of such dedicated, collective effort; and inspirations to wage an even more vigorous campaign to complete the unfinished business of racial justice. To be sure, the prospects for progress are more elusive and complex now than in times past, the visibility of Jim Crow having been replaced by the subtleties of institutional racism. But the price of resignation or complacency is high--too high.

Indeed, the positive observations on Black America in the 1990s are heavily outweighed by the negative aspects. Time and time again, the data document conditions and trends that do not augur well for the overall well-being of African Americans in the coming decades. Neglect or half-hearted remediations could spell veritable disaster.

In concluding the report, then, it is important to underscore our opening remarks on the broader context within which the information presented here gains meaning. In particular, the political mood of the country is distinctly less sympathetic toward the disadvantages of African Americans. Especially since 1980, we have witnessed widening promulgation and popularity of the view that the society is now "color-blind" and has met its constitutional obligations to ensure equality of opportunity for all. Contemporary racial disadvantages, the argument goes, are attributable to the failings of African Americans themselves--lack of motivation, dysfunctional social values, etc. Such sentiments have been much more than fodder for intellectual discourse. They have had eminently practical consequences for public policy.

Again, we are in an age of neo-conservatism regarding social issues. Thus, the federal government has drastically curtailed its role in supporting the aspirations of African Americans and other disadvantaged groups, leaving to the states the nature and extent of provisions for the needy. The federal disengagement, otherwise known as "devolution," has brought precipitous reductions in spending on targeted domestic programs. But the shift in governmental responsibility to states and localities has not been accompanied by a corresponding reallocation of the fiscal resources necessary to finance program initiatives. Consequently, many states have become very restrictive in their attitude toward meeting human needs, and Black Americans are being disproportionately impacted.

The recently enacted legislation on welfare reform stands as a prime example of the new policy perspective and its detrimental effects. Those who expected the Clinton Administration to restore and advance a progressive, enlightened commitment to the nation's domestic agenda have been very disappointed in this case, realizing that the swing to the right in political sentiment is not the exclusive province of the Newt Gingriches, Pat Buchanans, and Jerry Falwells of the world. It cuts across political parties, economic classes, and, yes, even race groups. Black conservatism, while still on the fringe, is an emerging phenomenon.

As mentioned, the adverse public policy developments have occurred alongside some disturbing trends within the black community itself. The problem of intra-group homicide and the more general phenomenon of crime in Black America persist with alarming frequency. Violent crimes among youth and illicit drug trafficking and abuse are blatantly deleterious and pervasive in their effects on African-American life. Similarly, the disproportionate incidence of teenage pregnancy frustrates the realization of human potential and prevents far too many black youth from taking advantage of such promising opportunities as are available.

If the overall black community is to survive and thrive in the face of such exigencies, it simply must take its destiny more into its own hands. It must dig deep into the potential of group effort on all fronts--political, economic, social, cultural--and dedicate its impressive resources to self-improvement. It must overcome the differences between generations and economic classes and recognize the primacy of the common good. It must determine to be more influential in the political, policy-making process, even as Black Americans re-energize the spirit of self-help and mutual support that is their legacy.

Viewed in terms of this assessment, this inaugural edition of *The Black Report* is an important tool, a resource to inform strategic designs, program initiatives, and outcome evaluations. We trust that data in subsequent editions of the *Report* will indicate significant movement toward meeting the formidable challenges that have been quantified and highlighted in these pages.